Amazing Animal Hunters

SHARKS

Jen Green

amicus

Published by Amicus
P.O. Box 1329, Mankato, Minnesota 56002

Printed in the United States of America at Corporate Graphics, in North Mankato, Minnesota.

Library of Congress Cataloging-in-Publication Data
Green, Jen.
  Sharks / by Jen Green.
     p. cm. -- (Amazing animal hunters)
  Includes index.
  Summary: "Discusses the life of sharks and profiles different types of sharks, along with providing facts
about habitat, diet, hunting practices, and more. Also includes records on sharks"--Provided by publisher.
  ISBN 978-1-60753-046-6 (library binding)
 1. Sharks--Juvenile literature. I. Title.
  QL638.9.G6944 2011
  597.3--dc22

                                                                          2009048514

Created by Q2AMedia
Editor: Katie Dicker
Art Director: Harleen Mehta
Designer: Dibakar Acharjee
Picture Researcher: Sujatha Menon
Line Artist: Parwinder Singh Soni
Coloring Artist: Danish Zaidi

All words in **bold** can be found in the Glossary on pages 30–31.

Web site information is correct at the time of going to press. However, the publishers cannot
accept liability for any information or links found on third-party web sites.

Picture credits
t=top b=bottom c=center l=left r=right
Cover images: Gerard Soury/Photolibrary, Ian Scott/Shutterstock

Chris and Monique Fallows/Photolibrary: Title page, Stephan Kerkhofs/Shutterstock: Contents page, Denis Scott/Corbis: 4,
Seapics: 7t, BW Folsom/Shutterstock: 7b, Aleksandrs Marinicevs/Shutterstock: 8, Don Bayley/Istockphoto: 9t,
Carnival/Shutterstock: 9b, Howard Hall/Photolibrary: 10, Jan Hinsch/Science Photo Library: 11t, Charles Hood/NHPA: 12,
David B Fleetham/Photolibrary: 13, Norbert Wu/Science Faction/Corbis: 14, Charles Hood/NHPA: 15t, Jonathan Bird/
Photolibrary: 15b, Ian Scott/Shutterstock: 16, Sergey Popov V/Shutterstock: 17t, Q2AMedia Image Bank: 17b, Cphoto/
Fotolia: 18, Seapics: 19t, Ryan M. Bolton/Shutterstock: 19b, Chris and Monique Fallows/Photolibrary: 20, A Soulas/Newspix/Rex
Features: 21, James Watt/Photolibrary: 22, Chris and Monique Fallows/Photolibrary: 23, John Chang/Istockphoto: 24,
Doug Perrine/Nature Picture Library: 25, Jurgen Freund/ Nature Picture Library: 26, Splashdown Direct/Photolibrary: 27,
Seapics: 28, Seapics: 29, Ian Scott/Shutterstock: 31.

Q2AMedia Art Bank: 5, 6, 11.

DAD0043
42010

9 8 7 6 5 4 3 2 1

Mississippi Mills
Public Library

Contents

Lords of the Ocean

Next time you visit the beach, ask any swimmer what creature they are afraid of. Most people will say sharks. Sharks are famous for their size, speed, strength, and razor-sharp teeth. They are also known as killers.

All Shapes and Sizes

Sharks are found in every ocean. They are fish (unlike whales and dolphins, which are **mammals**). There are about 400 **species** of sharks, of varying shapes and sizes. Some sharks are the size of a small yacht. Some are only as long as a pencil. Most sharks are torpedo-shaped, but some have flat bodies. Others have a blunt snout or a head like a hammer. Whatever their size, all sharks are meat-eaters, but some eat very tiny **prey**.

The great white shark is the world's most famous shark. It is known as a man-eater.

Pointed snout

Jaws are lined with sharp teeth

Sharks are a varied group of fish. Here are just a few examples.

Sawsharks have a long, narrow snout lined with teeth

Horn sharks have pig-like snouts

Angel sharks have a wide, flat body

Bamboo sharks are long and slender

Ancient Fish

Sharks have been around for an incredible 400 million years. They swam in the oceans long before dinosaurs walked on land. Since that time, the shark's shape has changed very little. This is because prehistoric sharks were already superbly suited to their watery world. Sharks differ from almost all other fish because their skeletons are made of rubbery **cartilage**, not bone. A group of flattened fish, called rays, are distant cousins of sharks. Rays have a skeleton of cartilage, too.

PREHISTORIC GIANT

Carcharodon megalodon was the largest flesh-eating shark that ever lived. This prehistoric killer had huge, dagger-shaped teeth 6 inches (15 cm) long, and probably measured about 60 feet (18 m) in length. Luckily, it became extinct about 1.5 million years ago!

Body of a Hunter

Sharks are unmistakable. Their pointed snouts, scary teeth, cartilage skeleton, and rubbery-looking skin all set them apart from other fish. You would easily recognize a shark from just a brief glimpse in murky water.

Skin and Skeleton

Cartilage is more bendy than bone. Having a cartilage skeleton makes the shark's body flexible. Your nose and ears are also made of cartilage, and can be gently bent from side to side. Cartilage is lighter than bone, which helps the shark to float. The shark's skin is also unusual. Most fish have smooth, rounded scales. The shark's skin is covered with tiny tooth-like scales called **denticles**. This makes it feel rough to touch. Sharks have been known to graze people and draw blood just by brushing against them.

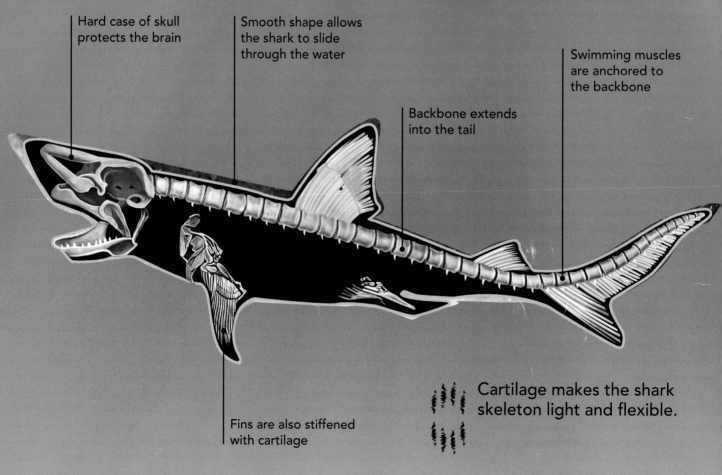

Hard case of skull protects the brain

Smooth shape allows the shark to slide through the water

Backbone extends into the tail

Swimming muscles are anchored to the backbone

Fins are also stiffened with cartilage

Cartilage makes the shark skeleton light and flexible.

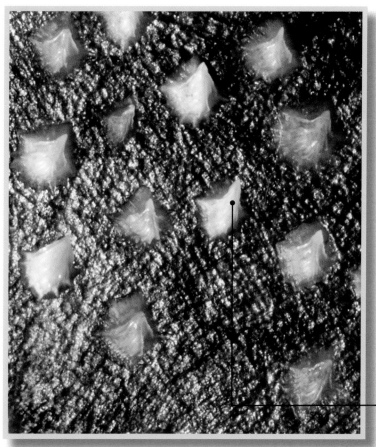

MOVING JAWS

The shark's powerful jaws can bite with enormous force. In some species, the jaws are loosely attached to the skull with stretchy **ligaments**. These sharks swing their jaws forward as they lunge at their prey.

Denticle has sharp point

Shark denticles are coated with enamel, like your teeth. In the past, shark skin was used as sandpaper.

Armed to the Teeth

A shark's main weapons are its teeth. Its enormous jaws contain up to 3,000 teeth, arranged in rows, one behind the other. The back teeth act as replacements for the working teeth in front. When a front tooth breaks off, a tooth from the second row moves forward to replace it. Sharks go through thousands of teeth in their lifetime!

Different types of shark have teeth of various shapes. Great white sharks and tiger sharks have dagger-shaped teeth with **serrated** (jagged) edges. Some sharks have long, pointy teeth, like needles, for gripping slippery fish. Others have blunt teeth for crushing hard-cased shellfish.

The great white shark has jagged teeth that act like steak knives, slicing through flesh and bone.

7

Watery World

Sharks are perfectly suited for the water. A shark's body is packed with muscle. It can dart through the water to overtake the fastest human swimmer. Unlike humans, sharks can breathe underwater using feathery structures, called **gills**.

Thrashing tail drives the fish forward

Large dorsal (back) fin keeps the shark stable

Pelvic and anal fins prevent the shark from rolling

Pectoral (chest) fins are used for steering and braking

Super Swimmers

A shark swims forward by throwing its body into S-shaped curves, powered by its thrashing tail. Fins help with steering and keep it stable. Many sharks have a tall, triangular back fin that sticks out of the water. This is a sure sign to swimmers that a shark is around. Other types of fish float with the help of a gas-filled organ called a **swim bladder**. Sharks don't have a swim bladder, but they do have a large liver filled with light oil, which helps them float. Even so, if a shark stops swimming, it will sink.

The thresher shark has a very long tail that makes up half of its body length.

Sharks have up to seven pairs of gill slits. This sand tiger shark has five.

Breathing Underwater

Like all fish, sharks breathe using gills. Most fish have a bony cover over their gills, but sharks have between five and seven gill slits on each side of their head. To breathe, the shark takes in oxygen-rich water through its mouth. As water flows over the gills, oxygen passes into a network of fine **blood vessels** and into the shark's bloodstream. Sharks have to keep swimming to breathe. If they stop moving forward they will drown.

SPEED FREAK

The blue shark is one of the fastest swimmers. It can speed along at 43 miles (69 km) per hour. Most sharks are "cold-blooded"— their body temperature is similar to the surrounding water. The fastest sharks can warm their muscles, brain, and other vital parts, which makes them extra-speedy.

Reef sharks rest on the seabed. They pump water over their gills so they can breathe while staying still.

Gills help the shark to breathe underwater

Basking Sharks

Basking sharks are among the very largest sharks, but you could swim alongside one without fear of attack. These gentle giants feed by cruising along at the surface with their huge mouths open. So what is their prey?

Floating Feast

Basking sharks are among the laziest creatures in the oceans. Instead of chasing prey, they swim along at a snail's pace and wait for food to drift into their mouths! They feed on floating creatures too small to see without a microscope. These tiny drifters include shrimp, fish eggs, and young crabs. Collectively known as **plankton**, they are plentiful in cold seas in spring and summer, coming to the surface in swirling clouds. Basking sharks swim to these food-rich waters to feast.

 Basking sharks are so called because they seem to bask in the sunshine at the surface. In fact, they are feeding on plankton.

Basking sharks are the world's second-largest sharks, growing to 33 feet (10 m) long and weighing up to 4.4 tons (4,000 kg)

Filter Feeding

If you tried to eat and breathe at the same time, you would choke, but basking sharks manage to do both at once! As they open their huge mouths, water swirls in and passes over the gills, where they take in oxygen. At the same time, giant bristles attached to the gills, called **gill rakers**, sieve out food. After about a minute, the shark closes its mouth. As water swirls out through the gill slits, the shark swallows its mouthful. By filtering about 400,000 gallons (1.5 million L) of water an hour—enough to fill a medium-sized swimming pool—the shark gets enough to eat.

These microscopic creatures are some of the plankton eaten by basking sharks.

Gill rakers are like giant combs made of bristly hairs.

Gill rakers strain off food

Gill filaments absorb oxygen from the water

Senses and Hunting

Sharks live by hunting. Many are flesh-eating **predators** that search out prey, such as seals and fish. Sharks will also eat dead animals and steal the kills of other hunters. Each of a shark's senses is finely tuned to track down its favorite prey—alive or dead.

Super Senses

Like humans, sharks have the five senses of sight, smell, hearing, taste, and touch. The shark's most important sense is smell. Sharks can detect a tiny trace of blood in the water up to a mile (1.6 km) away. The shark tracks the scent trail and then uses sight, hearing, and touch to close in for the kill. Sharks have some extra senses, too. A line of nerves running down the shark's sides, for example, picks up the vibrations of swimming creatures.

Super-keen nostrils are located on the underside of the snout

Little pits on the nose pick up electrical signals produced by swimming creatures at close range

Eyes see well in dim light

Most of the shark's senses are on its head.

Hunting Techniques

Different types of sharks use various tricks and techniques when hunting. Some sharks hunt in groups. The group spreads out to surround a **shoal** of fish and herd it into a tight ball. Then each shark dives into the ball to snatch a mouthful of fish. Other sharks hunt alone. Having tracked its prey, the shark circles around its victim to check if it is weak or injured, before lunging forward. Spinner sharks are so called because they spin around in the water to confuse their prey before they attack.

Sharks have three eyelids—an upper and lower lid—and an extra membrane that protects the eye as the shark attacks.

SWIMMING BLIND

As some sharks move in for the kill, a white eyelid closes over each eye to protect it from the teeth, claws, or spines of thrashing prey. Other species roll their eyes back in their sockets so that only the white eyeballs show.

Thick membrane for protection

The Amazing Hammerhead

The hammerhead shark is one of the most bizarre-looking creatures in the oceans. Its eyes and nostrils are located on the tips of its extraordinary T-shaped head.

Sensory pits on the snout pick up tiny electrical signals given off by swimming creatures

Wide head provides lift like an aircraft's wing. This prevents the shark from sinking

Chest fins

Tall dorsal (back) fin

Long tail thrashes to provide swimming power

Hammerheads have a large brain to process the data gathered from the senses on their wide head.

Hunting Tools

Hammerhead sharks swim in warm, tropical seas. Like all sharks, they are killers. They go after fish, squid, their cousins (skates and rays), and other sharks. Their hammer-shaped head evolved millions of years ago. The shark swings its head from side to side when hunting, as if using a metal detector. It can detect prey buried in the sand using its **electrosenses**. Scientists believe that having widely-spaced eyes and nostrils helps the sharks pinpoint their prey.

Varied Creatures

There are nine different types of hammerheads. The largest, the great hammerhead, measures up to 20 feet (6 m) long. The winged hammerhead has the widest hammer. The most common, the scalloped hammerhead, has a wavy edge to its hammer. Some female hammerheads live in quite large groups. They spend the day in a shoal of up to 100 sharks. They spread out at night to hunt and regroup at dawn. Imagine being out in a small fishing boat and being suddenly surrounded by these scary creatures!

Hammer is flattened from top to bottom so the shark can slide through the water

Widely-spaced eyes have a wide field of vision

Skin is sensitive to touch

STINGING PREY

Many hammerheads like to prey on stingrays. They don't seem to be harmed by the rays' long, poisonous stings.

Hunting Grounds

Sharks are found in many parts of the oceans. Most live in warm, tropical seas, but some patrol cooler **temperate** waters. The Greenland shark swims in the icy Arctic Ocean. Many sharks swim in the shallow waters around coasts, but some live far out at sea.

From Surface to Seabed

Many sharks hunt in the sunlit upper waters where there are lots of prey. These sharks often have dark backs and pale bellies. This coloring, called **countershading**, hides them against the dark depths or the sunlit surface. Sharks that live on the seabed, such as the wobbegong, have patchy markings that **camouflage** them against sand, rocks, and weeds on the ocean floor.

Coral reefs form in shallow tropical waters, where sharks can find prey such as fish.

Pale belly conceals this Caribbean reef shark against the sunlit surface from creatures looking up from below

Tassels look like seaweed to complete the shark's disguise

Blotchy colors blend with the rocks

Long-Distance Swimmers

Out to sea, sharks live at different depths in the water. We don't know much about deep-water sharks such as goblin sharks because these animals are rarely caught and studied. Some deep-water sharks make daily journeys up to the surface. They may spend the day in the depths and then rise to the surface to feed at night. Other sharks travel long distances through the oceans. Atlantic blue sharks can travel 15,000 miles (24,000 km) in a year.

FRESHWATER KILLERS

Bull sharks are known to swim up rivers, such as the Mississippi in America and the Congo in Africa. Unlike most sharks, they can survive in freshwater. They have been seen swimming about 2,500 miles (4,000 km) from the ocean. These very dangerous sharks have often attacked humans.

White fin tips give the shark its name

Dark back hides the shark against the blue depths below

Oceanic whitetips swim in the open ocean far from land.

17

Fearsome Tiger Sharks

Tiger sharks swim in tropical seas and warm temperate waters. They usually hunt in the shallow waters around coasts and islands. These are among the world's most deadly sharks—top predators of the seas, just as tigers are top predators on land.

Garbage Cans of the Sea

Some sharks are fussy about what they eat. Not tiger sharks! They target fish, squid, dolphins, seals, and seabirds. They will eat poisonous jellyfish and crunch hard-shelled turtles. Pet dogs, dead cattle, and deer have all been snapped up without a second thought. All sorts of **inedible** objects have also been found in tiger sharks' stomachs—ropes, hats, coal, cans, car tires, and license plates— even a whole chicken coop complete with chickens! For this reason, tiger sharks are nicknamed "the garbage cans of the sea."

Stripes provide camouflage

Tiger sharks are named for the tiger-like stripes running down their bodies. The stripes fade as the shark gets older.

Prowling Tigers

Tiger sharks are **solitary** hunters. They cruise around the oceans in search of their next meal. They regularly turn up off the islands of Hawaii, in the center of the Pacific Ocean, when large seabirds called albatrosses are breeding. When the young albatrosses take off for their first flight over the sea, the sharks are ready. They pick off any young bird that dips low over the surface. They will even leap up to snatch a flapping chick from the air.

A tiger shark quickly snatches a young albatross that comes too close to the water.

TIGER TEETH

Tiger sharks have unusual L-shaped teeth with sharp **prongs** and jagged edges. They sink their prongs into slippery prey such as fish. The jagged edges are used to slice through the flesh of creatures such as dolphins. The shark shakes its head to tear a chunk of flesh off its prey—much like tigers do on land.

Tiger shark teeth are strong enough to crush a turtle's shell.

Deadly Man-Eaters

Sharks have a reputation as man-eaters. However, most shark species are actually harmless as far as humans are concerned. Of 400 species, only about 30 have even been known to attack people. So are sharks really as bad as we make them out to be?

Shark Attacks

Every year, about 75 shark attacks are reported around the world. Of these, between 10 and 20 are **fatal**. Statistics show that far more people die from drowning, or after being stung by a bee. You are actually more likely to get run over by a car as you cross the road to the beach. The world's four most deadly sharks are great whites, tiger sharks, oceanic whitetips, and bull sharks. The coasts of Australia and Florida are particularly dangerous. On some beaches, nets keep the sharks away.

 Bull sharks are probably responsible for some attacks that are blamed on great white sharks.

The Wrong Victim?

Some shark attacks are probably cases of mistaken identity. Swimmers (especially divers in wet suits) look like seals—the favorite prey of many sharks—when glimpsed from below. A shark may also attack if it feels trapped or cornered. If you swim in waters where sharks have been seen, a few common-sense rules will help to keep you safe. Don't swim at night, which is when many sharks go hunting. Keep close to shore, and never swim off beaches where seals are breeding. Above all, don't swim if you have cut yourself—sharks have a super-keen nose for blood!

PLUCKY SURVIVOR

American surfer Bethany Hamilton was attacked by a tiger shark while surfing off Hawaii in 2003. The shark bit off her left arm. She was just 13 at the time. Plucky Bethany recovered and soon returned to surfing. She has since won major surfing championships and other awards.

Despite losing her left arm in a shark attack, Bethany Hamilton is a world-class surfer.

Great White Sharks

Great whites are the scariest creatures in the oceans. Their reputation as man-eaters was strengthened by the *Jaws* movies, which told how a great white terrorized a seaside town. But is this shark's reputation for ferocity really deserved?

White Death

Great white sharks are the world's largest predatory fish. They grow to 20 feet (6 m) long and can weigh 2.2 tons (2,000 kg). They swim in tropical and temperate seas in many parts of the world and have an incredibly powerful bite. Their huge size and strength make them particularly dangerous. Young great whites prey on fish and squid. Full-grown sharks feed on seals, sea lions, birds (such as penguins), other sharks—and the occasional human. They have also been known to attack boats.

Serrated teeth can slice through flesh and bone

Huge jaws contain up to 3,000 razor-sharp teeth

Great white sharks sometimes lunge right out of the water as they attack.

Crescent-shaped tail

FEEDING FRENZY

Filmmakers and scientists sometimes put out bait to attract great white sharks. A large quantity of food can cause many sharks to gather. The smell of blood makes the sharks enter a "feeding frenzy." They snap wildly, bite one another, and may even turn on one shark and tear it apart.

A great white shark is not white all over —the upper body is gray, brown, or blue

Cunning Hunters

Great white sharks are cunning hunters. They often swim up to their prey, take a large bite of flesh, and then move away for a while. When the victim grows weak from loss of blood, the shark moves in for the kill. Great whites target weak or injured prey rather than fit and healthy animals that put up a fight. Although the most feared sharks, they are actually only responsible for about 10 percent of attacks on humans.

Great whites are sometimes called White Pointers

A great white leaps from the water to snatch a seal.

Shark Babies

A shark's breeding habits are very unusual. Female sharks produce far fewer eggs than most other fish, but take much greater care of their unborn young.

Shark Eggs

Most female fish produce millions of eggs, but take little care of them. The female lays her eggs directly into water. The male sheds his **sperm** to fertilize the eggs. Then the parents swim off. Almost all the eggs are eaten by predators, and only a few survive to grow into adult fish. Sharks take much more care. The male uses a small fin called a **clasper** to transfer his sperm inside the female. A few types of shark, such as dogfish and catfish, then lay their fertilized eggs in the water. The babies grow up inside a tough, leathery case, nourished by the yolk.

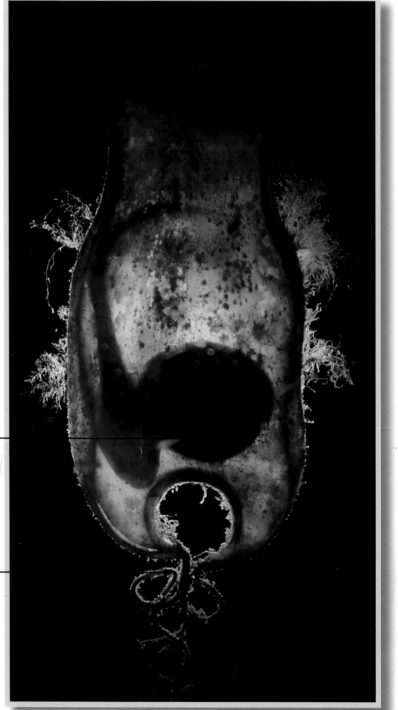

Yolk nourishes the baby dogfish

Curly tendrils anchor the case to seaweed

A young dogfish grows inside a leathery case called a "mermaid's purse."

Inside the Womb

Most baby sharks develop inside their mother's **womb**. The growing babies feed on yolk and sometimes unfertilized eggs. Unborn blue and hammerhead sharks are nourished by an organ called the **placenta**. Unborn tiger sharks and mako sharks are **cannibals**! The biggest **pups** feed on their smaller brothers and sisters in the womb, until just one or two big, fat pups are left. In all these sharks, the mother gives birth when the babies are fully developed. The pups are born tail first.

HOW MANY BABIES?

Sharks have varying numbers of young. Tiger sharks and mako sharks give birth to just one or two pups. Hammerhead sharks have up to 40 pups. The blue shark holds the record, giving birth to up to 135 pups! Some shark pups are born after growing for nine months inside the mother, just like human babies. Other shark pups take two years to be born.

This lemon shark is resting on the seabed as she gives birth.

Baby is fully developed at birth

Sharks in Danger

As top predators of the oceans, sharks have few enemies—except humans. Each year, sharks kill fewer than 20 people. Humans, on the other hand, kill millions of sharks. So who is the most deadly?

Hunted Creature

Sharks are mainly hunted for food. The "rock salmon" sold at seafood restaurants in Europe is actually spiny dogfish, a type of shark. In Japan and China, soup made from shark fins is very popular. Oil from shark liver is made into lipstick, skin cream, and medicines. Shark skin is used to make leather belts and bags. The cartilage is ground up into **fertilizer**. Shark teeth are used as jewelry. People also kill sharks for sport, or because they are frightened of them. Some sharks die after getting trapped in nets that have been put out to catch fish or to keep sharks away from beaches.

This fisherman is cutting off the fins of a shark to make into soup.

STUDYING SHARKS

We know very little about some sharks, because these dangerous, free-swimming fish are so difficult to study. Scientists sometimes study sharks underwater from the shelter of a metal cage. But sharks have been known to attack these cages! Scientists also fit radio tags to sharks so they can track their movements.

Save the Sharks

Many sharks are now scarce because of people. Sharks breed slowly, so their numbers don't recover if many of their kind are killed. Some sharks are in danger of dying out altogether. Today, more and more people are realizing that sharks need our protection. Sharks may not be cuddly, but they are still vital to the balance of life in the oceans. Many countries now limit the number of sharks their fishermen catch each year.

This fisherman is showing off the jaws of a shark he has caught.

Facts and Records

Sharks are record-breakers in many ways. They are top predators of the seas. Sharks are also among the rarest, fastest, and brainiest fish in the oceans.

Largest and Smallest

- The whale shark is the world's largest fish. It can grow up to 60 feet (18 m) long and weigh as much as two African elephants.

- Deep-water dogfish, as well as lantern and pygmy sharks grow to just 8 inches (20 cm) long.

You could pick up a pygmy shark in your hands.

The Rarest Shark

One of the world's rarest sharks is the megamouth shark. This deep-sea shark was only discovered in 1976. Since then, only a handful of megamouths have ever been seen. This rare shark grows to 16 feet (5 m) long. Its mouth measures 3 feet (1 m) wide. As a filter feeder, it cruises the ocean depths with its huge mouth open, sucking up shrimp.

Record-Breakers

- Thresher sharks have the longest tail of any shark, up to 8.2 feet (2.5 m) long.

- Mako sharks are one of the fastest sharks. Their speed helps them to leap 20 feet (6 m) above the water surface.

Body Facts

- Sharks can sense 1 part of blood in 100 million parts of water.

- Epaulette sharks have fleshy tentacles on their mouths. These are used to feel for prey buried in the sand.

- Frilled sharks are the skinniest sharks. They have eel-shaped bodies.

- Angel sharks are the widest sharks. They look as if they have been run over by a steamroller.

Did You Know?

- Small fish called shark-suckers (remoras) hitch a ride on a shark's rough skin and steal from its kill.

- The swell shark makes a noise a bit like a dog's bark.

- Although sharks are fast swimmers, they cannot stop quickly, and they cannot swim backwards.

- Tiny deep-sea lantern sharks give off light, so they glow in the dark depths.

Cookiecutter

A weird-looking shark called the cookiecutter has the largest mouth for its size. Its mouth forms a suction cup, which it uses to clamp onto its victims. It then twists around in a circle and rips off a round lump of flesh.

This dolphin has a circular scar left by a cookiecutter shark.

Glossary

blood vessel
a fine tube that carries blood around an animal's body

camouflage
the colors and patterns on an animal's skin, fur, or feathers that help it blend with its surroundings, so that it is hard to see

cannibal
an animal that eats its own kind

cartilage
the rubbery tissue that forms the skeleton of a shark

clasper
one of a pair of small fins used by male sharks for mating

countershading
when an animal is dark on top with a pale belly

denticle
one of the teeth-like scales of a shark

electrosenses
senses that use electrical signals

fatal
something that causes death

fertilizer
chemicals that farmers put on crops to make them grow

gill rakers
the bristles on the gills of some sharks that strain plankton from the water

gills
the feathery structures on a fish's head that allow it to absorb oxygen from water

inedible
something that should not be eaten

ligaments
stretchy, rope-like fibers that attach bones

mammal
an animal that feeds its young on milk and has hair on its body

placenta
a blood-rich organ that nourishes the unborn baby in mammals and also some sharks

plankton
microscopic animals
and plants that
provide food
for sea creatures
such as sharks

predator
an animal that hunts
others for food

prey
an animal that is
eaten for food
by another

prong
a sharp point

pup
a baby shark

serrated
having a
jagged edge

shoal
a group of fish

solitary
of an animal that
lives alone

species
a particular type of
animal, such as a
great white shark

sperm
a male sex cell

swim bladder
a gas-filled organ
that helps fish
to float

temperate
areas on Earth
lying between
the tropics
and the poles

womb
the organ in female
animals where an
unborn baby
develops

Index

Web Finder

Shark Research Unit
www.sharks.org/education_kids.htm
Find out how children have helped to save sharks.

Kidzone
www.kidzone.ws/sharks/facts.htm
Fun facts about sharks.

Seaworld
www.seaworld.org/infobooks/Sharks&Rays/home.html
All you need to know about sharks and rays.

San Diego Natural History Museum
www.sdnhm.org/kids/sharks/index.html
A web site packed with facts, games, and puzzles about sharks.

WWF
www.worldwildlife.org
Find out about sharks at risk from this conservation organization.